REVERIE

Whispers of the wandering mind.

Trupthi Ghorpade

BookLeaf Publishing

India | USA | UK

Made with ❤ on the BookLeaf Publishing Platform
www.bookleafpub.in
www.bookleafpub.com

Dedication

To my father, who bestowed upon me the finest education—not just in academics, but in the ways that truly shaped me. Though scholastic brilliance wasn't my forte, I found my rhythm in words, my strength in design, and my passion in all things unique. To my family, especially my mother and sister, for being my unwavering champions, nurturing every creative pursuit, and believing in my artistry even when I hesitated.
To my husband, my most discerning critic and steadfast pillar, who, in his own unvarnished way, anchored me to reality while still allowing me to dream. And to my girls, whose boundless love has been a luminous reflection of all that I am worthy of. You remind me, time and again, of the beauty of being a mother, the role I loved the most to play.

This book is for all of you my close knit friends and family—my foundation, my flight, my truth, and my 'reverie'.

Preface

Thoughts drift like clouds—sometimes fleeting, sometimes lingering. Reverie is a collection of such moments, woven into poetry that captures the ordinary yet profound essence of daily life. From quiet musings over morning coffee to the echoes of a passing conversation, these verses reflect the beauty in the mundane. They celebrate nostalgia, fleeting emotions, and the unexpected poetry hidden in routine. There is no grand narrative here—only snippets of thought, raw and unfiltered, yet deeply familiar. Each poem invites you to pause, reflect, and perhaps find a piece of yourself in these wandering reflections.

Let Reverie be your companion in stillness, a gentle reminder that even the simplest moments hold magic.

Acknowledgements

Creating Reverie has been a journey of reflection, inspiration, and gratitude. I would like to extend my heartfelt thanks to everyone who has been a part of this process.

To the countless experiences and everyday wonders that inspired these poems—thank you for teaching me to see beauty in the ordinary.

To my readers—this book is for you. May Reverie resonate with your own thoughts and emotions, reminding you that even the simplest moments hold poetry.

With gratitude,
Trupthi

Sun kissed

Upon my skin, dance the golden rays
A gentle warmth that seeps within.
So soft, so bright, the morning light,
My heart is filled with pure delight.

A golden glow, a tender touch
Sweet and slow. A kiss from sunshine.
The skies shine wide, and the breeze hums low
Joy as guide, what a perfect day to go.

The play of shadows, laughter sings,
All the nature wakes and how they spread their wings.
So fresh, so new, the world feels bright
Bathed in beams of golden sunlight

Carefree smiles and sun kissed cheeks
Days so bright that last for miles.
A grand gift for the day yet so simple,
A warm command with the sun's own touch.

Blue bae

White clouds so soft they drift slow and high,
Endless whispers floating through the bright blue sky.
Vast stretch of peaceful blue,
Sky a canvas in tranquil hue.

Sapphire light, the morning glows,
Day starts with gentle light, so pure, so bright.
In the noon your bold and free,
Like a dome boundless above the sea.

In shades so deep, in dusk you melt
Pink and gold together they sleep.
Still remains the endless sky,
With the stars awake, and the moon climbing high.

.

No chains no walls just cool air,
So sight the vast, beyond compare.
Calm and true, a piece of heaven,
Forever wide, forever a blue hue.

Missing warmth

Though the miles that keep us apart,
I miss you more is all I can say.
Every memory of your laughter lingers,
It lends a warmth in the quiet moments of my weary
days.
The simple joy of your presence I long,
The comfort of knowing you're near.
Though distance separates us,
I want you to know my dear
Love only grows for you no matter how far or near.

New love

The skies turned bright, after the storm
Love found me in the softest light.
The scars it left, I feared my past
Yet in your arms, I felt no theft.

When you made me laugh, my heart mended what was
torn,
Like dawn embracing a new night was reborn.
No longer was I lost in sorrow's of tide,
With you, now in my heart beats free, untied.

So warm, so true, Love came again,
A gentle start, a world brand new.

Again

She gives her all, She tries so true,
And yet every day, She starts anew.
Her efforts fade and words are all lost,
Unheard, unseen and at a heavy cost?

Her anger grows and fire burns
A storm within that only she knows.
Why should she fight to prove her worth
With sweat and tears have shaped my earth

Yet she stands though worn and torn,
She's a flame unbroken in a battle all worn.

Armor

Life's trials so dark and storms so wild,
I walk in faith, I'm your constant child.
Though weak each step I take, unsure,
Those mighty hands makes pathways pure.

Burdens weigh upon my chest,
You lift me up and make me whole.
The deepest pains and nights so long,
With your love become my song.

You are near in every test,
A guiding light, a place where I can rest.
No fear can break the trust I hold,
With your grace, my heart is always bold.

Lost treasures

Relics that time could not evade.
In the stalls they lye in sun and shade,
In a grand old hall, the clock that once chimed
A locket that held a love long gone.

Each dent, each scratch is a story untold,
Passed through ages, lost, then found,
Whispers of hands that once held them.
Silent keepers of secrets profound.

Who held them first? Who let them go?
Mysteries of these linger, and we'll never know.

Scars

The steady hands and beneath the bright smiles
Are scars time etched on shifting sand's?
Hearts worn thin, all silent warriors,
They march, straight up and they rise within.

Every wound has a story to tell,
Buried deep, yet never old.
No one see's the battles fought,
The price for staying strong, is the pain we brought.

With quiet a grace, still they stand,
Collecting new scars, recording them in books brand
new

Heartaches

Across the crowded street, I saw you
Time folded in, skipping a beat.
Your eyes still held that golden hue,
The love that I once swam through.

My laughter echoed from the days past,
Soft touches, that were meant to last.
Like an untamed tide memories surged,
Too sweet, too painful and sharp, too much to hide.

My heart ached and a headache bloomed behind my
eyes,
Love's cruel trick—what a beautiful lie.

Wrath

I silence the thunder, a storm brews within
Letting the embers burn under. Swallowing all the fire
Words pile up like waves that never break,
Thoughts like flood of fury in a quiet lake.

A sadness knocks, but I latch the door,
It seeps through the cracks in the floor.
I remain still, my voice remains light,
Yet inside, there's a rage in the night.

Screams of chaos that I force it to hide,
The war each day I fight with a smile outside.

Change

Like ocean tide, change rushes,
No place to run, no place to hide.
As the world moves fast, and it won't stand still,
Embrace, adapt or you'll lose your will.

Seasons change fast and time won't wait,
Your life will rewrite just what you create.
When new paths form and old ones fade,
Each step is a lesson, with each choice we make.

Fear may come in, doubt may call,
Don't fret change is growth—we rise, not fall.
Pen your arms, to face the new,
For life unfolds in shades of bright blue

My Miracle

At first when I held you, my heart stood still,
My miracle, soft and real.
Your fingers curled around my own,
Love so deep I'd never before known.

Sleepless nights and humming tunes,
Rocking you beneath the moon.
Every cry of yours and each little sigh,
Just filled my world with joy so high.

Being your mother, pure and true,
My dream came true the day I met you.

Lucky charm

My dream came true with you my second light,
Your a gentle soul, so warm, so bright.
I feared my heart was already full,
But as you arrived, you made me complete so beautiful.

Twice the laughter, twice the love,
My gift for life so pure from skies above.
With you, my love my dreams found space to grow,
A lucky charm, the true love I know.

You proved my heart could stretch so wide,
Forever yours, so full of pride.

Friendships

Years of laughter, tears, and fights,
We stood together, with wrongs made right.
Sometimes harsh words were spoken, tempers high,
But we never once said goodbye.

People and misunderstandings came and went,
Our love remained—unbreakable, unbent.
Life's highs and lows, through thick and thin,
We found our way back time and again.

True friendship isn't always rosy and smooth,
But time has only made us proof.

Mundane days

Chores and work, the clock moves slow,
Everyday life goes on, its steady flow.
Though moments blur, time never waits,
Every day is a thread, we weave our fate.

Sun still rises, the alarm still rings,
Yet another day of the same old things.
The world awakes, as the coffee brews
The same routine, the steps we take.

In simple days, in tasks we do,
Life goes on and hums along, both with old and new.

Amma

For my every wrong, through every fall,
Your love stood firm, forgiving all.
Your hands once soft, now worn with time,
Still reach for mine, still warm, still kind.

I strayed so far, yet in your eyes,
You give only love, no harsh goodbyes.
Your heart, is my home that never fades,
Your smile is the light that shines through all my shades.

Your always there no matter what, through dark or
bright,
Your love is my endless light.

Passion

Blazing like fire passion burns
Flying and lifting dreams ever higher.
A spark within, so bright and fierce
Making us cruise through our toughest time.

New hope ignites each new day,
Chasing all our doubts far away.
We all strive to build and grow,
For those we love, our hearts must show.

No limits bind the things we chase,
We carve a path, we set our pace.
Through every trial, we all stand tall,
With passion's flame, we never fall.

Nostalgia

I lived in golden days, once
In carefree haze, wrapped in love.
Childhood laughter echoed, soft and bright,
Safe beneath the stars in the night.

Worries never weighed upon my chest,
My tears were always laid to rest.
Hands to hold, no need to fight,
Parent's warm embraces felt so right.

Suddenly one day, the dream was done,
Life knocked out loud, and we had to run.
Sadness and fear, pain untold,
Very lonely even in the fold.

Love still remains, but it's not the same,
The child that I was, I miss before adult life came.

Strength

The nights feel cold, the world feels hollow and wide,
Now you're no longer by my side.
My pillar that stood, firm and tall,
The gentlest soul who knew it all.

The wisdom in you flowed like rivers deep,
Your words so calm, my fears would sleep.
It stilled my mind when it would race,
With talks and stories, love, and your grace.

Just silence lingers where you stood,
A space no one else could ever fill
I search for you in books you read,
In my thoughts, in dreams, and when in need.

Now you're not here, your voice remains,
My steady guide through happiness and pain.
Daddy your love still lights my darkest days,
You're the flame forever in my heart that time cannot
erase.

North star

So bright, a star that glows,
A soft whisper in the silent night.
She calls me forward, strong and true,
Through paths unknown and skies so blue.

Doubts arise and shadows fall,
Her steady light guides me through all.
Not seen by eyes, but felt within,
The voice that lifts, a fire akin.

However far I may roam,
She always leads me back to my safe home.

Me

She trusts their words, she feels them all,
Rises hope with each painful fall.
Her circle small, yet strong and true,
All know the storms that she's been through.

Her love too deep, she feels too much,
A heart so soft, a gentle touch.
Always giving, with endless grace,
Although fear still lingers in her space.

What a foolish heart, the world may say,
She still lets love lead her every way.
Always breaking, she bends, but never stays,
Rising up through darkest days.

For strength is all in the walls so high,
With the tears she lets run dry.
Through heartache's fire, she always stands,
She's a warrior's soul, with ever giving hands.